THE EASY AUTHENTIC
CHINESE COOKBOOK

WITH PICTURES OF EVERY STEP

Georgiana Kong

Contents

History

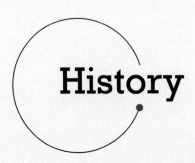

The "Cook Gene"

I was born in a large family full of talented cooks, my father being the most talented of all. With all the culinary arts happening in our home, I believe that I inherited the cook gene".

How I Got My Start

Although I enjoyed cooking, I did not do it as often as I liked until I got married in 2014. From that point, I cooked almost every day for our family and I fell in love with cooking!

Cooking requires practice, and it took me over 3-years to develop my skills. Now I truly enjoy making delicious and nutritious meals with minimal seasoning for my family.

I like collecting secret family recipes and try them immediately which turn out to be great! When I hold big family parties, I always got lots of accomplishments from my"critical"relatives , especially my mom.

Why I want to write a cookbook?

I had been working for an international adoption agency for almost 7 years, which has connected me with many adoption families and friends all over the world. After I posted a few cooking pictures on the internet, numerous people asked me to share the recipes so they too can make authentic Chinese food for their Chinese adoptive children.

I searched recipes on Google for simple and popular dishes in China, such as stir-fry Chinese spicy potatoes, tomatoes and eggs, but I was surprised that the recipes I found were not truly authentic. Therefore, I created a Facebook group for sharing my recipes. As the number of my followers grew, positive comments streamed in. As I reflected on the kids words I received, I decided to write this cookbook with the expressed goal of including popular and classic Chinese foods, but with easy to follow with step-by-step detailed instructions.

Dedication

To my beloved husband, Hu Yan, for his constant encouragement and untiring love.

To my dear friend, Brenda Eckel, a wonderful friend who patiently provided thoughtful suggestions throughout the writing of this cookbook.

To my precious father, Kong Ling Yu, from whom I inherited the family "Cooking Gene".

An Introduction to 12 'Must Have' Chinese Seasonings

After years of effort, I have come to realize how important it is to understand the use of seasonings for month-watering dishes. All of these seasonings can be found in the grocery store or on Amazon. My goal here is to provide information on the seasonings themselves and advice on how to use them.

1.Chinese Soy Sauce

Chinese Soy sauce is probably the best known traditional seasoning, and it is used in practically every cuisine . It is usually brewed for a few weeks with soybeans, salt, wheat, and water.

Light soy sauce is mainly used for cooking vegetables to add flavor, and it can also be served as a dipping sauce. It is a common staple in our household finding its way into nearly all my dishes. If you want a simple stir-fry, using the salt and light soy sauce will suffice.
Dark soy sauce is typically used for seasoning meat and for adding color to dishes.

2. Vinegar

Chinese white rice vinegar is made from fermented rice and is less acidic than Western distilled white vinegar. It is used for cooking pickles, salads, and stir-frying some vegetables such as tomatoes. A benefit of white vinegar is that it preserves the original color of the food.

Chinese black vinegar, with its enticing aroma, is more commonly used than rice vinegar . It is a dark complex, mild vinegar made of glutinous rice and malt. It is somewhat similar to a balsamic used in Chinese stir-fry, braises, and sauces.

Tip: The vinegar flavor is strong, so I recommend first-timers start with a small amount.

3. Sesame Oil

Sesame oil is an edible vegetable oil derived from sesame seeds. Besides being used as a cooking oil, it is used as a flavor enhancer in many cuisines, having a distinctive nutty aroma and taste.

It is mainly used as a marinade or added to dressings and dipping sauces. Please note, it is unsuitable for deep-frying due to its low boiling point.

4. Rice Wine (Shaoxing Wine)-Marinated Meat

Rice wine is made from sticky rice and millet, and is best used as a marinate for meats.

It is helpful in removing odors from meat and fish as well as improving the aroma of dishes by helping the flavors fully penetrate into the dishes.

5. Oyster Sauce

It is made from oyster extracts, sugar, salt, and water thickened with corn starch.

As a relatively new Chinese seasoning, I love using it when stir-frying vegetables. It is also widely used in numerous of dishes because its the sweet taste makes food taste fresh, especially vegetables.

6. Soybean Paste

Soybean paste has a distinctive salty and oily taste. I divided them into 2 kinds:

1) Spicy- red soybean paste. I strongly recommend Pixian bean paste, which is perfect for making Mapo Tofu and Red Cooked Beef.

2) Not Spicy- dark brown soybean paste. It is ideal for making Mao Dou Zha Jiang, a dish with dried tofu and beans.

7. Star Anise

Star anise is dark brown with eight prongs. Each has a black, shiny seed. It has a very strong, distinct flavor that is warm, sweet, and spicy, similar to licorice, fennel seed, clove, or anise seed, of course.

It plays an important role in slow-cooked dishes such as braised food.

8. Sichuan Peppercorn

Sichuan pepper is a spice from the Sichuan cuisine of China's southwestern Sichuan Province. It is said to benefit a person with a cold and aid a person with stomach discomfort. Its unique aroma and flavor is neither hot like chili peppers nor pungent like black pepper.

I do not use it often in typical dishes, but definitely for braised food. Some also use it for making Mapo Tofu.

9. Cornstarch

Cornstarch is widely used in cooking and baking. It is a pure starch powder that is extracted from corn kernels.

Marinated meat: Add the cornstarch directly to the meat with other seasonings, such as salt, Shaoxing wine, for tenderizing.

Thickener: Mixed the cornstarch with water, pour in at the end of cooking. Thicken the soup and lock the freshness and taste of the dish, such as cooking tofu. A dependable ratio is f 1 teaspoon cornstarch mixed with 1 tablespoon water.

10. Bay Leaves

The bay leaf is an aromatic leaf commonly used in cooking. It is not generally eaten but are rather simmered in a sauce or included in a braising liquid, and then removed before serving. Especially braised meat, usually cooked with Chinese cinnamon, Sichuan peppercorn.

11. Chinese Cinnamon

It is one of several species of Cinnamomum used primarily for their aromatic bark, which is used as a spice in braised dishes.

12. Dried Chili

It is widely used in Chinese cooking if you enjoy spicy food. Usually we cut the whole dried chilies into 2 or 3 parts and cook them with ginger and garlic cloves in heated oil to make fragrance first.

Chapter 1
Stir-Fry Dishes

Who can live without stir-fry dishes in China? They are quick and always appetizing. I choose the most authentic and popular stir-fry dishes such as cabbages, peppers, eggs, beef, beans, broccoli, shrimp, tomatoes and potatoes. After you gain experience with these ingredients, you can make most vegetables and meat stir-fry.

Chinese Potatoes and Peppers Stir-fry

Prep
10 mins

Cooking
5 mins

Servings
2

Love potatoes love this dish!

Ingredients:

★1 tablespoon cooking oil

★2 medium-sized potatoes

★3 dried chilies

★2 fresh green peppers
　(if you don't like spicy, use bell pepper)

★4 garlic cloves(sliced or minced)

★1 teaspoon fresh ginger(sliced or minced)

★2 teaspoons light soy sauce(divided)

★1/2 teaspoon white vinegar or black vinegar
　(white one is better for the color)

★1/2 teaspoon salt , or to taste

Instructions:

1 Peel the potatoes , and cut them into julienne strips. Regular grater is not recommended, the authentic way is using knife to cut. Trust me, taste better.

2 Rinse the potato strips under tap water to remove the excess starch, and then put them in the water to prevent oxidation. (The potatoes will get darker quickly without water).

3 Clean the green pepper, seed, and cut it into strips. Slice the garlic cloves and ginger . Cut dried chilies into 2-3 parts.

4 Heat up the wok on a high heat for about 40 seconds and pour in 1 teaspoon oil; after about 15 seconds (heat the oil), add garlic, ginger and dried chilies to stir -fry for about 15 seconds until fragrant, then add the green peppers. Turn the heat to medium high.

5 Add a teaspoon light soy sauce and quick stir-fry until the peppers begin to soften and smell fragrant. (This is a very important step to make the pepper yummy). Drain the potato strips very well and add to the wok, add 1/2 teaspoon salt , a teaspoon light soy sauce and a teaspoon white vinegar. (This is an important thing to make potatoes taste better). Stir-fry on a medium heat for 1 minute.

6 Taste before dishing out!

Tips

◆ Make sure to remove the excess starch of potatoes very well and put them in the water. Drain them thoroughly to cook!

◆ White vinegar is the secret seasoning for this dish.

◆ Always taste before dishing out! Start from the less amount of salt first. If the dish gets too salty, there is no good solution.

Chinese Potatoes and Sausages Stir-Fry

Prep
10 mins

Cooking
5 mins

Servings
3

Potatoes and sausages are Chinese kids' favorite food. So our smart parents cook them together to make this amazing popular dish!

Ingredients:

★1 tablespoon cooking oil

★2 medium-sized potatoes

★1 sausage(Shuang Hui Sausage in Asia market, if no, kielbasa sausage also works) or just pork bacon

★4 garlic cloves(sliced or minced)

★1 teaspoon fresh ginger(sliced or minced)

★2 teaspoons light soy sauce

★1/2teaspoon white vinegar or black vinegar (white one is better for the color)

★1/2 teaspoon salt, or to taste

Instructions:

① Peel the potatoes, and cut them into julienne strips.

② Rinse the potato strips under tap water to remove the excess starch. And then put them in the water to prevent oxidation. (The potatoes will get darker quickly without water).

④ Heat up the wok on a high heat for about 40 seconds and pour in a tablespoon oil, after about 15 seconds(heat the oil), then add garlic, and ginger; stir-fry for about 15 seconds until fragrant. Turn the heat to medium high. Drain the potato strips very well and add to the wok with sausage strips. Add 1/2 teaspoon salt , 2 teaspoons light soy sauce, 1/2 teaspoon white vinegar at the end (This is important to make potatoes taste better) and stir- fry on a medium heat for 1 minute.

Tips

◆Make sure remove the excess starch of potatoes and soak them in the water; drain them very well to cook.

◆White vinegar is the secret seasoning for this dish.

③ Cut the sausages into julienne strips. Slice the garlic cloves and ginger.

⑤ Taste before dishing out!

Chinese tomatoes and Eggs Stir-Fry

Prep
5 mins

Cooking
5 mins

Servings
2

It's the kind of dish that people say is the first thing they learned to cook, that fed them when they left home, that inspires sudden and irresistible cravings. When my hunger strikes, its always the first dish in my mind.

Ingredients:

★2 tomatoes

★3 eggs

★4 garlic cloves(finely chopped)

★2 tablespoons cooking oil

★1/2 teaspoon salt

★1 teaspoon light soy sauce

★3 teaspoons water

★1 scallion

How to peel tomatoes:

1) Cut a small cross on each tomato

2) Leave them under boiled water for 2 minutes

3) Take them out and pull the skin off when cool enough to touch. Remove the stems.

Instructions:

1. Peel off the skin of the tomatoes. Then cut them into chunks.

2. Break the eggs, and beat them with 3 teaspoons water (water makes eggs scramble). Finely chop the scallion and garlic cloves.

3. Heat up the wok with a tablespoon oil for about 1 minute on a high heat, pour the eggs in and stir slowly to make them into pieces. When eggs becomes solid, take out.

4. Heat up the wok with a tablespoon oil for about 20 seconds on a medium heat again, add finely chopped cloves until fragrant. (Cooking the garlic first is an important step for the stir-fry dishes). Add tomatoes, a teaspoon light soy sauce, and quick stir - fry for 1 minute on a medium heat.

5. Put back the eggs, add 1/2 teaspoon salt, and give them a quick stir for 10 seconds.

6. Taste and sprinkle the chopped scallions before dishing out.

Tips

◆ Choose the red and ripe tomatoes. Soft ones would be better.

◆ If you prefer more juice, Longer the cooking time in step 2 of how to peel tomatoes.

Scrambled Eggs and Peppers Stir-Fry

Prep
10 mins

Cooking
5 mins

Servings
3

Super simple ingredients- peppers and eggs, and super delicious!
It's always my first choice when I am busy or lazy.

Instructions:

① Break the eggs, and beat them with 3 teaspoons water (water makes eggs scramble). Clean the green pepper and drain well, seed and cut it into strips. Crush the garlic cloves and chop them with ginger into small pieces .

② Heat up the wok on a high heat for about 40 seconds and pour in a tablespoon oil, after about 45 seconds(heat the oil), then pour in the eggs. Stir slowly to make them into pieces when eggs becomes solid and take out.

③ Heat up the wok on a medium heat for about 10 seconds and pour in a tablespoon oil, after about 15 seconds(heat the oil), then add garlic and ginger and stir-fry for about 15 seconds until fragrant. Then add the green peppers.

④ Add 2 teaspoons light soy sauce and quick stir-fry until the peppers begin to soften and smell fragrant. (This is a very important step to make the pepper yummy). Put the eggs back in , add 1/2 teaspoon salt, and give a quick stir-fry for less than 15 seconds.

⑤ Taste before dishing out!

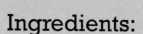

Ingredients:

- ★2 tablespoons cooking oil (divided)
- ★3 eggs
- ★2 fresh green peppers
- ★4 garlic cloves (sliced or minced)
- ★1 teaspoon fresh ginger (sliced or minced)
- ★2 teaspoons light soy sauce
- ★3 teaspoons water
- ★1/2 teaspoon salt, or to taste

Stir-Fried Cabbage

Prep
5 mins

Cooking
5 mins

Servings
2

A classic vegetarian version of Chinese stir-fry which is also healthy and weight watchers love.

Ingredients:

★ 2 tablespoons cooking oil half cabbage, 1 pound

★ 2 red chilies(Optional; if you don't like spicy, just skip)

★ 4 garlic cloves(sliced)

★ 1 teaspoon fresh ginger(sliced)

★ 2 teaspoons light soy sauce

★ 1/2 teaspoon white vinegar or black vinegar
   (white one is better for the color)

★ 1/2 teaspoon salt , or to taste

Instructions:

① Cut the cabbage into quarters. Then discard the stalk.

② Rinse the cabbage under the tap water and drain it very well.

③ Slice the garlic cloves and ginger. Cut dried chilies into 2-3 parts (optional; if you don't like spicy, just skip).

④ Heat up the wok on a high heat for about 40 seconds and pour in 2 tablespoons oil. After about 15 seconds(heat the oil), then add garlic, ginger, and dried chilies and stir-fry for about 15 seconds until fragrant. Then add the cabbage. Turn the heat to medium high.

⑤ Add 2 teaspoons light soy sauce and 1/2 teaspoon salt , then quick stir-fry until the cabbage begin to soften and smell fragrant. Add 1/2 teaspoon white vinegar, give a quick stir for 10 seconds.

⑥ Taste before dishing out! Good served with rice.

Tips

Discard the stalk. Quick stir-fry doesn't like the thick stalk which tastes worse.

Drain the cabbage VERY WELL. Water with cabbage would destroy the stir-fry.

Chinese Eggplant Stir-Fry

Prep
5 mins

Cooking
10 mins

Servings
3

One of the most difficult vegetables to cook? Takes longer time? Always ends up with eating much more oil?
Try my recipe, 15 minutes, less oil and amazingly delicious.

Ingredients:

★1 tablespoon cooking oil

★2 medium-sized eggplants

★4 garlic cloves (minced)

★2 teaspoons light soy sauce

★1 teaspoons dark soy sauce

★1 teaspoon salt, or to taste(divided)

★1 teaspoon oyster sauce

★2 tablespoons cornstarch

★1 scallion (chopped)

★1/2 teaspoon sugar

★1 bowl of water (about 1 cup)

◆Remove the excess water from the eggplant. This is a very important step for eggplant to absorb the seasoning better.

◆Taste in step 4, decide whether eggplant needs to cook longer (just add more water). It takes long time to cook through eggplant. Sometimes I add 2-3 times of water to cook.

◆Don't cut the eggplant thick. This will make it hard to cook through.

Instructions:

1 Cut the eggplant into similar size pieces (about 0.4 inches thick, 1 inches long) as the picture. Add 1/2 teaspoon salt , stir until each piece of eggplant is finely coated. Set aside for 5-10 minutes

2 Squeeze the eggplant very hard by hand to remove excess water; add 2 tablespoons cornstarch and mix well until the eggplants are evenly coated

3 Prepare a bowl. Mix together garlic cloves, 2 teaspoons light soy sauce, 1 teaspoon dark soy sauce, 1 teaspoon oyster sauce, 1/2 teaspoon sugar, and 1 bowl of water. Slice the garlic cloves and finely chop the scallion.

4 Heat the wok for 30 second on a medium heat and add a tablespoon oil; heat the oil for another 45 seconds, then add the eggplant. Give them a quick stir-fry until the eggplant becomes soft. Then pour in the mixed seasoning; add 1/2 teaspoon salt and cook for about 10-15 minutes on a low-medium heat until the eggplant are dry. Stir slowly if necessary.

5 Taste, sprinkle the chopped scallion and dish out. Good served with rice.

Beef and Pea Stir-Fry

Prep
15 mins

Cooking
10 mins

Servings
3

My daughter told me: "Serve me the beef and pea, and I can eat 2 bowls of rice!"

Ingredients:

★2 tablespoons cooking oil(divided)

★5 oz beef(sirloin or steak)

★1 bowl of peas

★1/2 carrot

★4 garlic cloves(sliced)

★1 teaspoon sliced fresh ginger

★2 teaspoons light soy sauce

★1 teaspoon dark Soy sauce

★1 teaspoon shaoxing wine or dry sherry

★1/2 teaspoon salt, or to taste

★1 teaspoon cornstarch

★1 teaspoon sugar or oyster sauce

Instructions:

1 Clean the beef: Soak beef in water for 5 minutes and knead for 1 minute to remove the blood. Drain well. (Blood in the beef would make the meat taste hard!) Mince the garlic cloves and ginger. Dice the carrot to similar size of 2 peas.

2 Marinate the beef: Dice the beef into small portions the similar size of 2-3 peas). Put the beef in a bowl, mixed with 1 teaspoon cornstarch, 1 teaspoon light soy sauce, 1 teaspoon dark soy sauce, 1 tablespoon cooking oil and 1 teaspoon shaoxing wine or dry sherry. Stir about 2 minutes to make sure all the beef is evenly coated. Set aside for 10 minutes.

3 Blanch the peas and carrot: Boil a bowl of water in the wok, add the peas after the water boils, take them out after 30 seconds. Cool with room temperature water, then drain them well. Set aside.

4 Heat up the wok on a medium heat for about 30 seconds and pour in a tablespoon oil, after about 10 seconds(heat the oil), then add the beef, quick stir-fry until the beef changes color (about 1 minute).

5 Add the peas and carrot, a teaspoon light soy sauce, a teaspoon sugar or oyster sauce , 1/2 teaspoon salt, and stir-fry for about 1 minute.

6 Taste before dishing out.

Tips

Peas are very tender, so blanch them quickly for no more than 30 seconds.

◆If you want the tender beef, always remember to remove the blood from it!

Beef , Pepper, and Edamame Stir-Fry

It's a very CREATIVE dish. You can use chicken or pork instead of beef. Or just pepper and meat stir-fry; pepper and edamame stir fry. All taste amazing!

Ingredients:

★2 tablespoons cooking oil(divided)

★5 oz beef(sirloin or steak)

★1 bowl of edamame (optional)

★1 fresh pepper(seeded)
  (Red pepper is good for the color)

★4 garlic cloves(sliced)

★1 teaspoon sliced fresh ginger

★2 teaspoons light soy sauce

★1 teaspoon dark Soy sauce

★1 teaspoon shaoxing wine or dry sherry

★1/2 teaspoon salt , or to taste

★1 teaspoon cornstarch

| Prep 15 mins | Cooking 10 mins | Servings 3 |

Tips

◆If you want the tender beef, always remember to remove the blood from it!

◆Why It's Important to slice beef against the grain

-----It's not just the cut of beef that determines how tender it is, it's also how you cut the beef. First, find the direction of the grain(which way the muscle fibers are aligned), then slice across the grain rather than parallel with it.

◆Blanching the edamame should be quick. No more than 40 seconds. Cool with room temperature water to keep them fresh.

Instructions:

1. Clean the beef: Soak beef in water for 5 minutes and knead for 1 minute to remove the blood. Drain well. (Blood in the beef would make the meat taste hard!)

2. Marinated the beef: Cut the beef into shreds against the grain. Put the shredded beef in a bowl, mixed with 1 teaspoon cornstarch, 1 teaspoon light soy sauce, 1 teaspoon dark soy sauce, 1 tablespoon cooking oil, and 1 teaspoon shaoxing wine or dry sherry. Stir about 2 minutes to make sure all the beef is evenly coated. Set aside for 10 minutes. Clean the pepper and drain, seed and cut it into strips. Slice the garlic cloves and ginger.

3. Blanch the edamame: Boil a bowl of water in the wok, add the beans after the water boils. Take them out after 40 seconds (softens the beans). Cool with room temperature water, then drain them well. Set aside.(if you don't have edamame, skip this step)

4. Heat up the wok on a medium heat for about 30 seconds and pour in a tablespoon oil, after about 10 seconds (heat the oil), then add the beef, quick-stir fry until the beef changes color (about 1 minute) and take out.

5. Heat up the wok on a medium heat with a teaspoon oil, after about 15 seconds(heat the oil), then add garlic and ginger, stir-fry for about 15 seconds until fragrant; then add the peppers and edamame. Add a teaspoon light soy sauce and stir-fry for about 1 minute. Add the beef and 1/2 teaspoon salt, give them a quick stir-fry for about 40 seconds.

6. Taste before dishing out!

Dried Tofu and Peppers Stir-Fry

Prep
5 mins

Cooking
10mins

Servings
3

It's one of the most popular homemade dishes in every Chinese family. We eat it about 60 times a year!

Ingredients:

★2 tablespoons cooking oil

★5 oz Dried Tofu
   (The fresh dried tofu I use is not salty)

★2 fresh green peppers

★4 garlic cloves(sliced)

★1 teaspoon sliced fresh ginger

★2 teaspoons light soy sauce

★1 teaspoon dark soy sauce

★1 teaspoon oyster sauce

★1 teaspoon salt(divided), or to taste

◆Dried tofu absorbs the salt and
   seasoning very slow (just like tofu).
   So step 3(blanch) is very essential.
   If you use the salty dried tofu, skip
   step 3.

◆If you like spicy, use the spicy
   pepper. If not, just use the bell
   peppers. Both delicious. My 2 years
   old daughter loves the bell pepper.

Instructions:

① Slice the dried tofu, garlic cloves and ginger. Clean the green peppers, seed and cut it into strips.

② Blanch tofu: Boil 2 bowls of water with 1/2 teaspoon salt (if your dried tofu is salty, no salt here). Add the dried tofu until the water boils. Cook the dried tofu for 1 minute , then take out and drain. (This step is for tenderizing and salting the dried tofu). Prepare a bowl, mixed with 1 teaspoon dark soy sauce,1 teaspoon oyster sauce, 1/2 teaspoon salt, and 3 tablespoons water.

③ Heat up the wok on a medium heat for about 10 seconds and pour in a tablespoon oil, after about 15 seconds(heat the oil), then add sliced garlic and ginger and stir-fry for about 15 seconds until fragrant. Then add the dried tofu and pour the seasoning from the bowl, stir-fry for about 2-4 minutes until tofu gets dry. Add the pepper strips and 2 teaspoons light soy sauce. Stir-fry until the pepper get a little soft.

④ Taste before dishing out!

Easy Shrimp and Broccoli Stir-Fry

Prep
10 mins

Cooking
10 mins

Servings
3

Just shrimp and broccoli--Damn Delicious!

Ingredients:

★2 tablespoons cooking oil

★5 oz shrimp

★10 oz broccoli

★4 garlic cloves(sliced)

★1/2 teaspoon sliced fresh ginger

★2 teaspoons light soy sauce

★1 teaspoon oyster

★1/2 teaspoon salt , or to taste

Marinate shrimps ingredients:

◆1 tablespoon Shaoxing Wine or dry sherry

◆2 teaspoons cornstarch

◆1/2 teaspoon salt

◆1/2 teaspoon sliced fresh ginger

◆1 teaspoon ground black pepper

Instructions:

1. Slice the ginger and garlic cloves. Marinate the shrimp: Clean the shrimp and put in a bowl. Mix well with 1 teaspoon shaoxing wine or dry sherry, 2 teaspoons cornstarch, 1 teaspoon ground black pepper, 1/2 teaspoon salt and 1/2 teaspoon sliced ginger. Set aside for 10 minutes.

2. Cut the broccoli into small parts. Blanch them in boiled water for about 1 minute. Take out and drain well.

3. Heat the wok with 2 tablespoons cooking oil on a medium high heat for about 30 seconds; add garlic cloves and stir-fry for about 30 seconds until smells fragrant. Add the shrimp, and 1 teaspoon dark soy sauce. Stir-fry until the shrimp change color. Add the broccoli and 1/2 teaspoon salt, 2 teaspoons light soy sauce and 1 teaspoon oyster sauce. Stir-fry for about 2 minutes on a high heat.

4. Taste before dishing out!

Tips

◆ Bigger and fresh shrimp taste much better.

◆ Broccoli absorbs the salt very slow, so we like to blanch it first.

Broad Beans
and Eggs Stir-Fry

Prep
10 mins

Cooking
10 mins

Servings
3

Broad bean dishes are always fresh. It is the No.1 broad bean dish--easy to follow and super tasty!

Ingredients:

★1 bowl of broad beans(about 6 oz)

★3 eggs

★4 garlic cloves(sliced)

★2 tablespoons cooking oil(divided)

★1/2 teaspoon salt

★2 teaspoons light soy sauce

★2 bowls of water about 2 cups and
   3 teaspoons water (divided)

Instructions:

1. Break 3 eggs and beat them with 3 teaspoons water. Slice the garlic gloves.

2. Blanch the beans: Boil 2 bowls of water in the wok, add the beans after the water boils , take them out after 40 seconds (Softens the beans). Cool with room temperature water, then drain them well. Set aside.

3. Heat up the wok with a tablespoon oil for about 1 minute on a high heat, pour the eggs and stir slowly to make them into pieces. When eggs becomes solid, take out.

4. Heat up the wok with a tablespoon oil for about 20 seconds on a medium heat again; add sliced garlic cloves until fragrant, add beans, 2 teaspoons light soy sauce, and quick stir - fry for 1 minute on a medium heat.

5. Put the eggs back in; add 1/2 teaspoon salt, and give them a quick stir for 10 seconds.

6. Taste before dishing out.

Chapter 2
Steamed Dishes

As a mom, I fall in love with steaming food because they are popular among kids and super easy Prepare. I affectionately refer to them as "Lazy mom's dishes".

Although steamed eggs is the most difficult dish in this cookbook, I encourage you to be brave and try my recipe; you can make it easily and flawlessly.
Steamed pork and pork ribs are kids favorites because they are so tender!
Steamed edamame is so authentic and healthy.

Chinese Steamed Eggs

Prep
5 mins

Cooking
10 mins

Servings
3

In China, we have an old saying: Steaming an egg , tells whether or not you are a good cook. Try my secret recipe, you can make one which is better than restaurant!

Chinese steamed eggs requires minimum ingredients yet unbelievable flavor; but it's not easy to make it flawlessly.

Ingredients:

★1 teaspoon sesame oil

★3 eggs

★95°F warm water . The amount of water is 2 times the volume of the eggs. So if you have 200 milliliters of egg, you could use 400 milliliters of water.

★3 teaspoons light soy sauce

★1/2 teaspoon Black Vinegar (Eggs like Vinegar. Vinegar always makes eggs tasty. (Don't add more, because vinegar has very strong taste)

★1/2 teaspoon salt

★2 scallions (finely chopped)

◆If you don't have a steamer , DIY with a bamboo steamer.

◆Set aside for 20 minutes. Cover the eggs very well to steam.--Key Step

◆This is a recipe you need to follow precisely. The time of steaming should be no more than 8 minutes after water boils.

◆This is my secret family recipe for several generations.

Instructions:

1. Break the eggs; add 1/2 teaspoon salt, 3 teaspoons light soy sauce, 1/2 teaspoon black vinegar, and 2 times amount of eggs of warm water. Whisk them very well. You would find out there are so many bubbles on the top(also many bubbles inside which you can't see). SET ASIDE for 20 minutes.

2. After 20 minutes, if there are still some bubbles. Remove them by using a filter.(Bubbles will make your eggs rough and full of little holes after steaming).

3. Finely chop the scallions. Cover the plate with aluminum foil or plate. (I use a plate...easier way). This step is to prevent any water droplets from the steamer from falling directly onto the eggs, making the surface of the steamed eggs rough.

4. Steam the covered eggs for 8 minutes after water boils. Add a teaspoon sesame oil and sprinkle the chopped scallion on the surface. (You can also sprinkle the scallions on the egg before steaming which is my favorite taste).

 Looks so pretty and Serve warm.

Steamed Pork Ribs

Prep
20 mins

Cooking
1 hour

Servings
3

**No.1 of Pork Ribs Dish,
Lazy mom loves it,
Kids love it,
We all love it!**

Ingredients:

★1 scallion(finely chopped)

★14 oz pork ribs

★6 garlic cloves(minced)

★1 teaspoon sliced ginger

★2 teaspoons light soy sauce

★1/2 teaspoon salt(or to taste)

★2 teaspoons dark soy sauce

★1 teaspoon oyster

★2 teaspoons cornstarch

★1 teaspoon Shaoxing Wine
  (or dry sherry)

★2 teaspoons sesame oil

Instructions:

1. Slice the garlic cloves and ginger. Chop the scallions.

3. Move the pork chops in a plate and steam it for 1 hour on a medium heat.

2. Clean pork ribs. Cut them into 2 inches long. Marinate the pork ribs: Put them in a large bowl, mixed with a teaspoon Shaoxing wine(or dry sherry), 1/2 teaspoon salt, 2 teaspoons light soy sauce, 2 teaspoons dark soy sauce, 1 teaspoon oyster, 2 teaspoons cornstarch, and 2 teaspoons sesame oil. Stir and mix well to make sure all the ribs are evenly coated. Set aside for 15 minutes.(This step is the soul of the dish-to tenderize and flavor the pork ribs)

4. Taste and sprinkle with the scallions. Serve with warm.

Tips

◆ To make them tender and tasty, Just steam it for a longer time!

Steamed Pork with Rice Flour

Prep
20 mins

Cooking
40 mins

Servings
3

Two years ago, We have a popular news about an American come to China 3 times with her daughter just for this super delicious dish! However, you can make it anywhere with my recipe.

Ingredients:

★1 scallion chopped

★12 oz pork belly

★4 garlic cloves (sliced)

★1 teaspoon sliced ginger

★6 tablespoons rice flour

★2 teaspoons light soy sauce

★1/2 teaspoon salt

★2 teaspoons dark soy sauce

★2 teaspoons cornstarch

★1 teaspoon Shaoxing Wine (or dry sherry)

★2 teaspoons oyster

★2 teaspoons sesame oil

Instructions:

 Clean the streaky pork. Cut them into thin slices.(about 3/4 inch thick) .Marinate the pork:Put them in a large bowl. Mixed with a teaspoon Shaoxing wine(or dry sherry), 1/2 teaspoon salt, 2 teaspoons light soy sauce, 2 teaspoons dark soy sauce, 2 teaspoons cornstarch, 2 teaspoons oyster, 6 tablespoons rice flour and 2 teaspoons sesame oil. Stir and mix well to make sure all the pork are evenly coated. Set aside for 15 minutes.(This step is the soul of the dish--tenderize and flavored the pork)

 Move the pork in a plate and steam it for 40-50 minutes.

Taste and sprinkle the chopped scallions. Serve with warm.

Tips

◆Choose the pork with fat taste much better. Pork belly is the most classic and popular choice.

◆To make them tender and tasty, steam it longer time for 1 hour on a medium heat.

Steamed Edamame

Prep
2 mins

Cooking
20 mins

Servings
3

Edamame has a special amazing taste, so we love to keep the original taste, cook it in the simplest way. You will be surprised when taste this popular homemade dish!

Ingredients:

★7 oz Edamame

★1/2 teaspoon salt(to taste)

★3-4 garlic cloves(sliced)

★1 teaspoon light soy sauce

★1 teaspoon sesame oil

★2 teaspoons boiled water (optional)

Instructions:

1 Clean the 7 oz edamame and drain well. Don't take away the white skin of edamame because its healthy and make the dish tasty. Chop or slice the garlic cloves . Add them to the edamame.

2 Steam it for about 20 minutes. Then add a teaspoon light soy sauce,1 teaspoon sesame oil, 2 teaspoons boiled water(optional), and 1/2 teaspoon salt immediately. Stir and mix well.

3 Taste and dish out. So yummy! So fresh!

Tips

◆ Don't add more water in step 3 ...more water would destroy the dish totally!

Steamed Edamame with Fresh Pepper

Prep
4 mins

Cooking
20 mins

Servings
3

It's from my father -in- law...a very talented cook in our big family. It's his secret recipe for a person who loves spicy food.

Ingredients:

★7 oz Edamame

★1 fresh green pepper(spicy)

★1/2 teaspoon salt(to taste)

★3-4 garlic cloves(minced)

★1 teaspoon light soy sauce

★1 teaspoon sesame oil

Instructions:

1 Clean the 7 oz edamame and drain well. Don't take away the white skin of edamame because its healthy and makes the dish tasty. Mince the garlic cloves. Add them to the edamame. Clean the pepper and drain. Slice the seeded pepper.

2 Steam the edamame for about 10 minutes; add the pepper. Then continue to steam for another 10 minutes. Add 1 teaspoon light soy sauce,1 teaspoon sesame oil and 1/2 teaspoon salt immediately. Stir and mix well.

3 Taste and dish out.

Tips

◆ Pepper makes it special for the person who like spicy. The fresh pepper is the soul.

◆ I love to use instant pot to steam it when steam rice.

Chapter 3
Cold Dishes and Salad

Cold dishes are popular and welcome in summer. They are also must-serve dishes in Chinese festivals and holidays.

You will find my family secret recipes of cucumber, century eggs, daikon radish, apple and tofu. They are all easy to follow and taste amazing.

Sweet Cucumber with Apple - Tastes Like Cantaloupe!

Prep
5 mins

Cooking
10 mins

Total
15 minutes

What happened when a cucumber meets an apple-- Becomes a cantaloupe!
Yes, it would taste like cantaloupe.
But not exactly the same taste.
We all love it in summer.

Ingredients:

★1 medium-sized cucumber
★8 tablespoons sugar
★1 medium-sized apple

Instructions:

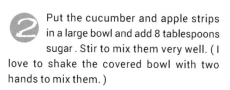
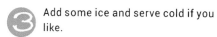

1 Peel the cucumber and apple, and cut them into strips.(You can first slice and then cut into strips).

2 Put the cucumber and apple strips in a large bowl and add 8 tablespoons sugar . Stir to mix them very well. (I love to shake the covered bowl with two hands to mix them.)

3 Add some ice and serve cold if you like.

Tips

The peeled apples would get oxidation quickly. The color would be a little bit gray on the surface.

Century Eggs with Tofu Salad

Prep
15 mins

Cooking
3 mins

Servings
18

◆It's the only dish that I order every time in any restaurant .

◆Thousands of years authentic Chinese dish.

◆On the top list of classic and popular cold dishes.

◆My recipe beats the restaurants!

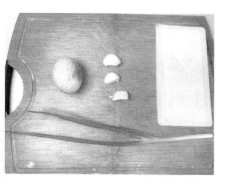

Instructions:

Ingredients:

★2 tablespoons sesame oil

★1 package (16 oz / 450 g) of silken tofu

★2 century duck eggs

★4 garlic cloves(finely chopped)

★1/4 teaspoon salt

★1 teaspoon minced ginger

★2 tablespoons light soy sauce

★1 tablespoon black vinegar

1 Take the silken tofu out of the package and put block on a plate. Steam the silken tofu for 10 minutes after the water boils. If you find there is some water on the plate, pour the water off and let tofu set until it is cool enough to touch. Then sprinkle 1/4 teaspoon salt on the tofu.(Most people doesn't know this step, but it's the secret to make silken tofu tasty.)

3 Heat 2 tablespoons sesame oil on a wok or a small frying pan for 20 seconds on medium heat; add the finely chopped garlic cloves and ginger. Stir about 15 seconds until smells fragrant; add 2 tablespoons light soy sauce and a tablespoon black vinegar, do a quick stir for 5 seconds and pour on the surface on the tofu and eggs.

Tips

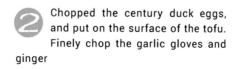

◆Tofu needs to be steamed for removing the excess water.

◆Stir-frying the chopped garlic cloves and ginger makes seasoning fragrant.

2 Chopped the century duck eggs, and put on the surface of the tofu. Finely chop the garlic gloves and ginger

4 Set aside until cold and enjoy!

Quick Pickled Daikon Radish

Prep
20 mins

Cooking
12 hours

Servings
12 hours and
20 minutes

Every time I want to make a pickle, Daikon radish is always my priority. Because it is so quick to make, and so tasty to match any food.

Ingredients:

★1 medium-sized fresh daikon radish

★3 spicy red peppers(optional)

★3 garlic cloves(sliced)

★2 teaspoons light soy sauce

★2 teaspoons salt

★9 tablespoons sugar

★5 tablespoons white vinegar

★2 tablespoons sesame oil

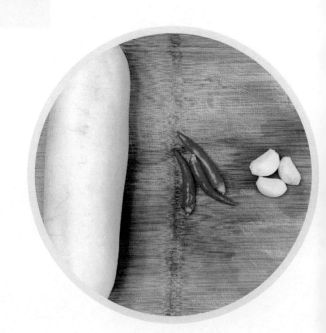

Instructions:

① Peel the daikon radish, and cut it into strips.(You can first slice and then cut into strips). Slice the garlic cloves and spicy red pepper.

② Put the daikon radish in a large bowl and add a teaspoon salt; stir well to make sure all daikon radish strips are coated. Set aside for 15 minutes. (This step is to remove the water from daikon radish and make them absorb the seasoning quickly)

③ Marinate the daikon radish: add 1 teaspoon salt , 2 teaspoons light soy sauce, 9 tablespoons white vinegar, 5 tablespoons sugar, and 2 tablespoons sesame oil. Stir to mix them very well.

④ Cover the bowl with plastic wrap , refrigerate and marinate 12 hours or overnight before serving.

Tips

Choose the fresh daikon radish. The skin should be smooth, and it should feel heavy.

◆ If you like spicy, it would be very appetizing.

◆ We like to refrigerate the pickled daikon for 2 days. It tastes better!

Simple Tofu Salad with Scallions

Prep
5 mins

Cooking
10 mins

Total
15 mins

Instructions:

1 Finely chop the scallions and mince the garlic cloves. Cut the soft tofu into 1/2 inch squares.

2 Blanch the tofu: Add tofu with 1/2 teaspoon salt into the boiling water for about 5 minutes under the medium heat. Take tofu out and drain well.

Ingredients:

★2 tablespoons sesame oil

★1 package of Soft Tofu (about 15 oz)

★5 scallions(chopped)

★4-6 garlic cloves(finely chopped)

★2 teaspoons light soy sauce

★1 teaspoon ground black pepper

★1 teaspoon oyster sauce

★2 teaspoons Dou Ban Jiang(Pixian Bean Paste is the recommend one)

★1 teaspoon salt , or to taste (divided)

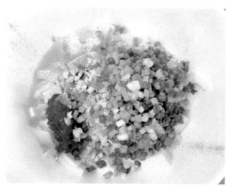 

3 Transfer the tofu in a big bowl, add 1/2 teaspoon salt, 2 teaspoons light soy sauce, 1 teaspoon ground black pepper, 2 teaspoons Bean Paste, a teaspoon oyster sauce, minced garlic and chopped scallions.

4 Heat 2 tablespoons sesame oil on medium heat for 1 minute. Then pour in the tofu bowl immediately (I like the sound when pouring).

 Mix well and serve either hot or warm.

Smashed Cucumber Salad

Prep 15 mins	**Cooking** 3 mins	**Total** 18 mins

◆Chinese people cannot live without it in summer.

◆Healthy; Weight watchers love.

Ingredients:

★2 teaspoons sesame oil

★2 cucumbers

★1 tablespoon roasted peanuts(minced) (optional)

★4-6 garlic cloves(finely chopped)

★3 tablespoons light soy sauce

★3 tablespoons black vinegar

★2 dried chilies(optional)

★1/2 teaspoon salt

Instructions:

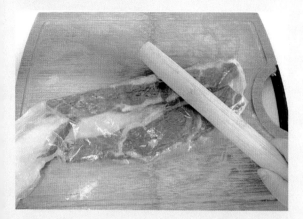

1 Cut off the top and the bottom of the cucumber(don't need them). Smash the cucumber inside a sealed plastic bag to keep the seeds from flying everywhere. Take the cucumber out, cut into cubes.

3 Finely chop the garlic cloves. Mince the roasted peanuts. Put the chopped garlic cloves and minced peanuts in a bowl; add 2 teaspoons sesame oil, 3 tablespoons light soy sauce, and 3 tablespoons black vinegar. Mix them very well and pour on the cucumbers. Set aside for 10 minutes.

2 Sprinkle 1/2 teaspoon salt on cucumbers, and stir well to make all of them coated with salt. Set aside for 10 minutes. (This step is for removing the excess water from cucumber).

Tips

◆You can add some ice or put it in the refrigerator at the end to make cucumbers even colder and crunchier if you like.

Chapter 4
Braised Dishes

I f you search well-known Chinese foods, they are always braised dishes. It is a time-consuming process and requires some special skill to cook.

Everyone loves a great beef dish, and when you add the blend of seasonings and spices I recommend in the recipes, your family and friends will thank you at dinner time!
You can also try Mapo tofu and Kung Pao Chicken. Many people tell me my recipes beats ones found at a restaurant.
Glass noodle one is my personal favorite.

Authentic Simple Mapo Tofu

Prep
15 mins

Cooking
20 mins

Servings
3

●If you like both spicy food and tofu, this is the ideal one!
●Most recipes need so many ingredients and are hard to follow, but if you find the soul ingredient and secret step , it's actually simple and so appetizing.

Ingredients:

★1 package of Soft Tofu (about 15 oz)

★4 oz ground meat(pork or beef)

★1 scallion (chopped)

★6 garlic cloves (minced)

★1 teaspoon light soy sauce

★1 teaspoon dark soy sauce

★1 teaspoon salt

★2 teaspoons cornstarch

★3 tablespoons spicy fermented bean paste
(Pixian bean paste is the recommend brand, it's the soul of the dish. You can find it on Amazon or Asia Store)

★1 bowl of water about 1 cup

Instructions:

(3) Mix 2 teaspoons cornstarch and a tablespoon water in a bowl. Set aside.

(1) Cut the soft tofu into 1/2 inch squares, put them in the boiled water, add a teaspoon salt. After 5 minutes, take the tofu out and put them in the water to cool and drain well.

(4) After 10 minutes, (stir the cornstarch first because it sinks to the bottom quickly); pour 1/3 mixed cornstarch water in the wok, and stir slowly, after 1 minute, pour another 1/3 mixed cornstarch water in the wok, and stir slowly, after 1 minute, pour the rest 1/3 and stir(3 times of adding mixed cornstarch water which is the secret step for hundreds of years. Don't mix all at once). Cook until the tofu gets dry.

(2) Heat the wok for 30 seconds on a medium heat and add a tablespoon oil for 10 seconds (heat the oil), then add the ground meat and a teaspoon light and dark soy sauce; quick stir-fry until the meat changes the color; add the minced garlic cloves. Stir-fry for 30 seconds until smells fragrant, add 3 tablespoons Pixian bean paste and 1 bowl of water. Then put back the tofu to cook.

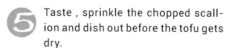

(5) Taste , sprinkle the chopped scallion and dish out before the tofu gets dry.

Tips

- The first step is crucial to make tofu tasty, remove the raw taste of tofu, and make tofu absorb the salt first. (Tofu absorbs salt very slowly)
- The forth step,3 times of adding cornstarch water, don't skip it. (Cornstarch is the secret of Chinese cooking, and in this dish especially).

Chinese Braised Chicken

Prep
10 mins

Cooking
1 hours

Total
70 mins

A delicious authentic Chinese recipe and only exists in China
●One of the greatest Chinese cooking techniques in the history yielding countless regional variations; but it is also one of the must-served dishes in Chinese festival meals.
●The aroma is the key.

Slow Braising Ingredients:

★2 tablespoons dark soy sauce

★2 tablespoons light soy sauce

★1 tablespoon rock sugar

★4 star anise

★4 bay leaves

★2 teaspoons salt

★1 stick Chinese cinnamon

★2 dried chilies(optional)

★1/2 tablespoon Sichuan peppercorn

★1/2 green onion(sliced)

★1 teaspoon sliced ginger

★Water as needed

Ingredients:

★10 chicken wings and 10 chicken thighs

★2 teaspoons Shaoxing wine or dry sherry

★1 teaspoons sliced ginger

★1/2 green onion (sliced)

Instructions:

1 Clean the chicken wings and thighs and drain well. Put them into the cold water to steam with 2 teaspoons Shaoxing wine or dry sherry, 1 teaspoon sliced ginger and some sliced green onion. Boil for 5 minutes. Remove the foam on the top.

2 Transfer the chicken wings and thighs to a large pot or instant pot. Add all the slow braising ingredients and enough cold water to cover them. Bring to a boil on a high heat and then simmer for 40 minutes on a small heat. (If you use instant pot, just press porridge button to cook until finished.)

3 Serve them warm. So tender and delicious.

What else can be braised?

---So many! Beef shank, pork butt, peanuts, dried tofu and dried bean curd. Popular and must-served dishes in Chinese big festival.

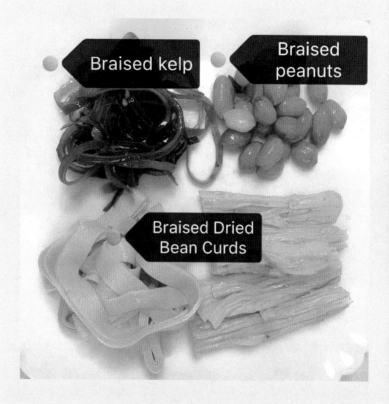

Braised kelp   Braised peanuts

Braised Dried Bean Curds

● For braising the meat, like beef shank, pork butt, chicken, all you need to do is the first and second step. Beef takes longer time to braise, sometimes 1 hour to steam and soak for 4-6 hours.

● For braising peanuts and dried tofu, just soak in the braised soup for 12-24 hours after turning off the heat.

● For braising dried bean curd, soak in the cold water for 20 minutes until curds are soft. Then soak them in the braised soup for 12 hours after turning off the heat.

Kung Pao Chicken --Royal Court Dish

Prep
25 mins

Cooking
15 mins

Servings
4

Famous thought the world!
But do you know It's the royal court dish in China?
Try my easy to follow recipe that tastes as good as royal!

Ingredients:

★3 tablespoons cooking oil

★1 fresh cucumber

★1 fresh carrot

★1 tablespoon roast peanuts

★7 oz boneless chicken breast

★4 garlic cloves(sliced)

★1 teaspoon sliced fresh ginger

★2 teaspoons light soy sauce

★1 teaspoon dark soy sauce

★1/2 teaspoon salt, or to taste

★1 teaspoon cornstarch

★1/2 cup of water

★1 teaspoon oyster sauce

Marinate chicken ingredients:

★1 teaspoon ground black pepper

★1 teaspoon cooking oil

★1/2 teaspoon salt

★1 teaspoon Shaoxing Wine(or dry sherry)

★1 teaspoon cornstarch

Instructions:

① Marinate the chicken: Cut the chicken breast into small cubes. Put them in a bowl, mix well with a teaspoon cooking oil, a teaspoon cornstarch, 1/2 teaspoon salt, a teaspoon Shaoxing wine (or dry sherry), a teaspoon ground black pepper, make sure all the cubes are evenly coated. Set aside for 20 minutes. (This step is for tenderizing the chicken and removing the raw flavor).

② Prepare a tablespoon roasted peanuts. Slice the garlic cloves and ginger. Peel the carrot. Dice the carrot and cucumber.

③ Prepare a bowl, mixed with 2 teaspoons light soy sauce, 1 teaspoon dark soy sauce, 1 teaspoon black vinegar, 1 teaspoon oyster sauce, and 1/2 teaspoon salt. Set aside.

④ Heat up the wok on a medium heat for about 30 seconds and pour in 2 tablespoons oil, after about 10 seconds (heat the oil), add the chicken breast, stir- fry for about 1 minute until the chicken changes color. Take them out. Set aside.

⑤ Heat up the wok with 1 tablespoon oil on a medium heat for about 20 seconds, add the sliced garlic and ginger to stir fry until smells fragrant (about 20 seconds). Add the mixed seasoning of Step 3. Add carrot, cucumber, chicken, and 1/2 cup of water to the wok, cook them for about 10-15 minutes to get dry.

⑥ Taste before dishing out.

Tips

If you like spicy, you can add spicy pepper or dried chilies.

Ground Pork with Tofu

Prep
15 mins

Cooking
40 mins

Total
55 mins

If you dislike spicy food but are a tofu lover, this is ideal.
Most recipes need so many ingredients, and are hard to follow. Try mine, it will surprise you!

Ingredients:

★1 package of Soft Tofu(about 15 oz)

★2 tablespoons cooking oil

★4 oz ground meat(pork)

★1 scallion(chopped)

★6 garlic cloves(minced)

★1 teaspoon light soy sauce

★1 teaspoon salt(divided)

★1 teaspoon dark soy sauce

★1 teaspoon oyster

★2 bowls of water

Marinade ground pork ingredients:

★1/2 teaspoon salt

★1 teaspoon cornstarch

★1 teaspoon dark soy sauce

Instructions:

1 Cut the soft tofu into 1/2 inch squares, put squares into the boiled water; add 1/2 teaspoon salt. After 4 minutes, take the tofu out and put squares in the water to cool, and drain well.

2 Marinate the ground pork: stir and mix well the ground pork with 1 teaspoon dark soy sauce, 1/2 teaspoon salt, and 1 teaspoon cornstarch. Set aside for 5 minutes.

3 Heat the wok for 30 seconds on a medium heat and add 2 tablespoons oil for 10 seconds (heat the oil), then add the ground meat and a teaspoon light soy sauce, quickly stir-fry until the meat changes color; add the minced garlic cloves. Stir-fry for 30 seconds until smells fragrant; add a teaspoon dark soy sauce, a teaspoon oyster sauce, and 2 bowls of water .

4 Put the tofu back into wok and cook. Turn to the medium-small heat after the tofu in the wok boils. Add 1/2 teaspoon salt and a teaspoon light soy sauce. Continue to cook about 45-60 minutes until the tofu gets dry.

5 Sprinkle the chopped scallion and taste before dishing out.

Tips

◆The first step, blanching, is crucial for making the tofu tasty. It removes the raw taste; and salt the tofu a little. (Tofu absorb salt very slowly)

◆Cook the tofu longer time under a small heat so it will be more tasty. Sometimes I cook for nearly a hour. Just add more water to prevent tofu from getting too dry.

Mao Dou Zha Jiang

Prep
15 mins

Cooking
25 mins

Servings
4

It's a very old and authentic Chinese food. Kids love it when not spicy. Adults are crazy about it when spicy.

Ingredients:

★2 tablespoons cooking oil

★1 cucumber

★1 carrot

★7 oz boneless chicken breast

★5 oz dried tofu

★6 oz green soy bean (Edamame) (1 bowl)

★Half onion

★4 garlic cloves(sliced)

★1 teaspoon sliced fresh ginger

★1 tablespoon light soy sauce

★2 teaspoons dark soy sauce

★1 teaspoon salt, or to taste

★1 bowl of water 〔about 1 cup 〕

★1 teaspoon oyster

★3 tablespoons Dou Ban Jiang

(if you like spicy, use Pixian Bean Paste).

If for kids or not spicy, just skip this)

Marinate chicken ingredients:

★1 teaspoon Shaoxing Wine(or dry sherry)

★1/2 teaspoon salt

★2 teaspoons cornstarch

★1 teaspoon ground black pepper

★1 teaspoon cooking oil

Instructions:

1 Marinate the chicken: Cut the chicken breast into small cubes. Put them in a bowl, mixed well with 1 teaspoon cooking oil, 2 teaspoons cornstarch, 1/2 teaspoon salt, a teaspoon Shaoxing wine (or dry sherry), a teaspoon ground black pepper, make sure all the cubes are evenly coated. Set aside for 20 minutes. (This step is for tenderize the chicken and remove the raw flavor)

4 Heat up the wok on a medium heat for about 30 seconds and pour in 2 tablespoons oil, after about 10 seconds(heat the oil), then add the chicken breast, stir-fry for about 1 minute until the chicken changes color. Add carrot, beans, onion, and tofu to the wok. Stir-fry for a minute. Then add a bowl of water, a tablespoon light soy sauce, 2 teaspoons dark soy sauce, a teaspoon oyster, 3 tablespoons of Dou Ban Jiang. Cook for 20 minutes on a medium heat just before it gets dry.

3 Boil a bowl of water in the wok, add the beans after the water boils. Take them out after 40 seconds (Softens the beans). Then cool with room temperature water; drain them well. Set aside.

2 Slice the garlic cloves and ginger. Peel the carrot. Dice the carrot, dried tofu, and onion.

5 Taste before dishing out. Perfect served with rice and noodles.

Minced Pork with Glass Noodle

 Prep 25 mins

 Cooking 10 mins

Total 35 mins

A mouth-watering recipe that you must try. Also, it is quick and easy.

Ingredients:

★4 oz ground meat(pork or beef)

★4 oz glass noodles

★1 teaspoon minced ginger

★4 garlic cloves (minced)

★2 tablespoons cooking oil

★1 teaspoon light soy sauce

★1 teaspoon dark soy sauce

★1/2 teaspoon salt

★1 tablespoon spicy fermented bean paste (Pixian is the recommend brand, its the soul of the dish. You can find it on Amazon)

★1 teaspoon oyster sauce

★3 bowls of hot water

★1/2 teaspoon salt

Instructions:

1 Soak the glass noodles in the hot water (boiled water temperature) for 15 minutes. Prepare a bowl: Stir and mix with a teaspoon dark soy sauce, a teaspoon oyster, and 1 tablespoon of Pixian spicy fermented bean paste and 3 tablespoons water. Set aside.

2 Heat the wok for 30 seconds on a medium heat and add 2 tablespoons oil for 10 seconds (heat the oil), then add the ground meat and a teaspoon light soy sauce; quickly stir-fry until the meat changes color; add the minced garlic cloves. Stir-fry for 30 seconds until smells fragrant; pour in the seasoning from the bowl.

3 The glass noodles should be soft by now. Take out from the water.(Use scissors to give them a few rough cuts. If the noodles are too long, they will stick together while cooking.) Add to wok with 1/2 teaspoon salt and stir for 30 seconds. Continue to cook until the glass noodles are transparent and soft.

4 Taste before dishing out. Serve warm.

Tips

◆ Glass noodle is tasty, but not easy to cook. They absorb the seasoning very quickly and stick together when they get cold. Serve warm.

◆ To avoid glass noddles getting sticky when cook, please remember to blanch them with room temperature water after soaking in the hot water.

Red Cooked Beef

Prep
10 mins

Cooking
2 hous

Total
2 hours and
10 mins

There is extremely famous beef restaurant in our city sells over 1 million dollar of beef dishes in one year! Here is the secret recipe. After you try it, you would figure out why.

Instructions:

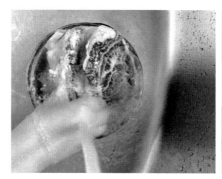 

1 Slice the ginger and garlic cloves. Clean the cilantro and drain well. Soak the beef in the water for 1 hour to remove the blood. Then rinse the beef to clean it and drain. Cut the beef into two parts.

Ingredients:

★3 tablespoons cooking oil

★2 pounds beef (select a fatty, well-marbled piece of stew meat)

★1 bunch of cilantro

★1 cinnamon stick

★6 bay leaves

★2 teaspoons sliced ginger(divided)

★4 big sliced garlic cloves(divided)

★2 black cardamom

★6-8 dried chilies(divided)

★2 teaspoons salt(to taste)

★4 teaspoons light soy sauce

★2 teaspoons shaoxing wine or dry sherry

★2 teaspoons dark soy sauce

★3 teaspoons oyster

★1 teaspoon sugar(3 rock sugar is better)

★3 tablespoons Pi Xian Broad Bean Paste (My Secret Sauce)

2 Put the beef in the wok or pot along with the 1 teaspoon sliced ginger, beef and 2 sliced garlic cloves, 1 cinnamon stick, 6 bay leaves, 2 black cardamom, 3-4 sliced dried chilies and enough water to cover the beef completely. Bring to a boil over a high heat. Then turn to a small heat to continue cook for 1 -2 minutes. Turn off the heat. Cover with lid for 10 minutes.

3 Take the beef out and cut it into small chunks until cool enough to touch. Remove the soup to the big bowl and the aromatics on the plate.

④ Heat the wok with 3 tablespoons oil for 1 minute under a small heat; add the rest of sliced ginger, garlic cloves and dried chilies, 1 teaspoon sugar, 4 teaspoons light soy sauce, 2 teaspoons shaoxing wine, 3 teaspoon oyster and 3 tablespoons Pi Xian Broad Bean Paste and the beef to stir fry for 1 minute, then add 2 teaspoons dark soy sauce and the aromatics to stir fry for about 5 minutes under a low-medium heat until the beef is dry. Add 2 teaspoons salt and give them a quick stir-fry.

⑤ Pour all the soup to the wok over the edge of the wok(as the picture shows). Cover the lid to bring to a boil under a high heat. Then turn to the medium heat to cook for 30-40 minutes (taste in the middle to see whether needs more salt). Turn off the heat and set aside for 30 minutes covered with a lid.

⑥ Serve warm with fresh cilantro. Save the beef soup because it can be used for Beef noodles, Beef Hot Pot...anything you want to cook with.

Chapter 5
Instant Pot Dishes

We love rice, and we love the instant pot. The instant pot is a great invention for a busy wife and/or mom who wants to make delicious food quickly and easily.

I am sure your kids will love Cola Chicken and Instant Pot Rice almost as much as you will! It is a good choice for your children's school lunch, and it is super easy to make.

Cola Chicken Wings (Instant Pot)

Prep
50 mins

Cooking
25 mins

Total
75 mins

Popular for over 30 years in China.
Every child wants to taste it just
when hearing the name. Hugely
popular in Hong Kong.
You'll be surprised by the unique
taste !

Ingredients:

★1 tablespoon cooking oil

★8 chicken wings

★1oz sliced fresh ginger

★2 teaspoons light soy sauce

★1 teaspoon dark soy sauce

★1/2 teaspoon salt , or to taste

★1 can of coca cola

Instructions:

1 Clean the chicken wings and drain well. Cut the skin of the chicken wings as pictured. (Chicken with cuttings can absorb the seasoning better). Marinate the chicken wings with a teaspoon dark soy sauce, 2 teaspoons light soy sauce, 1 tablespoon cooking oil and 1/2 teaspoon salt. Mix well and set aside for 40 minutes.

2 Slice the ginger and put slices in the bottom of instant pot. Add chicken wings on the ginger and pour a can of cola (to cover the chicken). Press the rice button and start .

3 Just cook the same way as you cook rice for instant pot. After about 25 minutes, dish out and serve warm.

Tips

It's a super easy recipe. The most important thing is cutting the skin of the chicken wings to absorb the seasoning better.

Instant Pot Rice
with Mushrooms

Prep
10 mins

Cooking
25 mins

Total
35 mins

Lazy mom loves it.
A perfect easy and quick way for making dinner or lunch.

Ingredients:

★2 teaspoons cooking oil
  (sesame oil is better)

★1 cup of rice

★1 small potato (5oz)

★1/2 bowl of corn kernels

★1/2 carrot

★2 oz of sausage (salty with meat)

★3 mushrooms

★2 teaspoons light soy sauce

★1 teaspoon dark soy sauce

★1 teaspoon oyster sauce
  (optional)

★1/2 teaspoon salt or to taste

Instructions:

1 Wash the rice and drain well. Put in the instant pot. Peel the potato and carrot. Dice potato, carrot, mushrooms and sausage (slice or dice).

2 Add them with corn kernels and 1 cup of water to the instant pot. Press rice button and start.

3 When finished, add 2 teaspoons light soy sauce, 1 teaspoon dark soy sauce, 1 teaspoon oyster sauce, 2 teaspoons oil and 1/2 teaspoon salt. Mix well.

4 Taste and dish out.

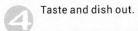

Tips

◆It.s a very creative recipe. You can add vegetables you like. Sausages are optional, it can be vegetarian or use meat to instead of sausages. Just remember marinate the meat first.

Instant Pot Rice with Vegetables and Sausage

Prep
10 mins

Cooking
25 mins

Total
35 mins

Lazy mom loves it.
A perfect easy and quick way for making dinner or lunch.

Instructions:

 Wash the rice and drain well. Put in the instant pot. Peel the potato and carrot. Clean the tomato (Cut a cross on the top).

② Dice potato, carrot and sausage (slice or dice).

③ Add them with corn kernels, tomato and 1 cup of water to the instant pot. Press rice button and start.

④ When finished, add 2 teaspoons light soy sauce, 1 teaspoon dark soy sauce, 1 teaspoon oyster sauce, 2 teaspoons oil and 1/2 teaspoon salt. Mix them well.

⑤ Taste and dish out.

Ingredients:

- ★2 teaspoons cooking oil (sesame oil is better)
- ★1 cup of rice
- ★1 small potato (5oz)
- ★1/2 bowl of corn kernels
- ★1/2 carrot
- ★2 oz of sausage or bacon (salty with meat)
- ★1 small tomato or half tomato (too much tomato would make the rice sour)
- ★2 teaspoons light soy sauce
- ★1 teaspoon dark soy sauce
- ★1 teaspoon oyster sauce (optional)
- ★1/2 teaspoon salt or to taste

Tips

The perfect proportion of rice and water is 1:1.2 by volume, but It's 1:1 in this recipe because tomato has lots of juice.

◆You can also use chicken, pork, or beef to instead of sausage. Just remember to marinate meat first.

Chapter 6
Noodles (Chow Mien vs. Lo Mien)

What is the next option if you are not in the mood for rice? For most Chinese, it would be noodles. I include some popular noodle dishes.

Classical Chow Mien

Prep
5 mins

Cooking
5 mins

Servings
3

Chow mein are Chinese stir-fried noodles with vegetables and sometimes meat.

Many people are huge Chow Mien fans, --such as my husband. It is particularly popular throughout the Chinese restaurants.

Want to make it?

Try my recipe, use the everyday ingredients and it beats most restaurants.

Ingredients:

★3 tablespoons cooking oil
   (divide; sesame oil is better)

★10 oz chow mien noodles
   (or ramen noodles)

★2 eggs

★4 garlic cloves(finely chopped)

★2 pieces of bacon

★6 bok choy stalks

★2 scallions (finely chopped)

★2 teaspoons light soy sauce

★1 teaspoon dark soy sauce

★1 teaspoon salt , or to taste

★1 teaspoon sugar

Instructions:

① Cook 10 oz chow mien noodles in a large pan of boiling water for 3-5 minutes, stir them constantly to prevent the noodles from sticking together. Then drain and put them in cold water. Drain thoroughly, then toss them with 1 tbsp sesame oil and set aside.

② Whisk 2 eggs and stir fry in pan with 1 tablespoon oil, then take out. Set aside.

③ Chop the garlic cloves and slice the bok choy and bacon.

④ Heat up the wok on a medium heat for about 20 seconds and pour in 2 tablespoons oil, after about 15 seconds(heat the oil), then add chopped garlic and stir -fry for about 15 seconds until fragrant. Then add bacon and bok choy, 1 teaspoon dark soy sauce, 2 teaspoons light soy sauce and stir fry for about 2 minutes until smell fragrant.

⑤ Add the noodles, eggs, 1 teaspoon sugar and 1 teaspoon salt; stir-fry for about 5 minutes on a medium heat.

⑥ Taste before dish out!

Tips

How to get chow mien noodles?

◆ You can get them in Asia store. Usually they have phrase "chow mien noodles" on the package. If not, use just ramen noodles or instant noodles without seasoning packs!

◆ It's a very creative dish. You can use cabbage instead of bok choy; use chicken or beef (marinate fresh meat first) instead of bacon; or add mushrooms and bean sprouts. All taste amazing!

Shanghai Scallion Oil Noodles

Prep
5 mins

Cooking
8 mins

Servings
3

◆It was love at first bite, and I knew I had to share it with you. After trying my recipe, you will find out how ridiculously easy it is to make!

◆The restaurant version had ground pork in it, but I decided to take it out and make our scallion oil noodles vegetarian friendly.

Ingredients:

★2 teaspoons light soy sauce

★1 teaspoon salt or to taste

★2 teaspoons dark soy sauce

★2 tablespoons sesame oil

★1 teaspoon sugar

★6 scallions (chopped)

★0.5 pound dried thin noodles

Instructions:

1. Remove the white part of scallions. We only want the green part. Finely chop the green part. Boil 2 bowls of water, add the noodles after the water boils. Stir slowly to prevent noodles from sticking together. After about 5 minutes, transfer the soft noodles in a big bowl. Rinse in cool water to cool down and drain well. Add 2 teaspoons light soy sauce, 2 teaspoons dark soy sauce, 1 teaspoon sugar, chopped scallions and 1 teaspoon salt.

2. Heat the 2 tablespoons sesame oil in pan on medium heat for 1 minute, then pour the hot oil to the bowl immediately. Stir and mix them well.

3. Taste and dish out.

Tomato Egg Noodles

Prep
5 mins

Cooking
5 mins

Servings
2

Chinese kids's first bowl of noodle

Ingredients:

★1 tablespoon cooking oil

★1 big tomato

★2 eggs

★1 scallion(chopped)

★2 teaspoons light soy sauce

★2 bowls of water

★1 teaspoon salt , or to taste

★0.5 pound dried thin noodles

Instructions:

Make the soup first:

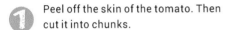

① Peel off the skin of the tomato. Then cut it into chunks.

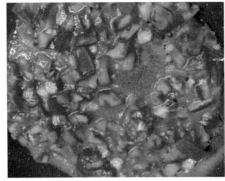

③ Heat up the wok with a tablespoon oil for about 1 minute on a high heat, add the tomato, stir fry for a minute until the juices come out.

② Break the eggs and beat them. Finely chop the scallion.

④ Add 2 bowls of water, leave it until the water boils. Pour the eggs into the wok; stir slowly to spread the eggs. When the eggs become solid, add 1/2 teaspoon salt and 2 teaspoons light soy sauce.

Make the noodles:

① Boil 2 bowls of water, add the noodle after the water boils. Stir slowly to prevent noodle from sticking together.

② After about 4 minutes, move the noodles to the tomato soup bowl. Add 1/2 teaspoon salt. Sprinkle the chopped scallions .

③ Taste and dish out.

Tips

◆ Always add noodles after the water boils.

Chapter 7

Rice, Congee, Egg Pancakes and Tea Eggs

also would love to share some breakfast and dinner recipes with you. 20minutes to make the congee! 10 minutes egg pancakes! And authentic tea eggs with minimum ingredients, fried rice, etc...

How to Make Congee in 20 Minutes -with Great Consistency

Prep
5 mins

Cooking
20 mins

Total
25 mins(not including the refrigerator time)

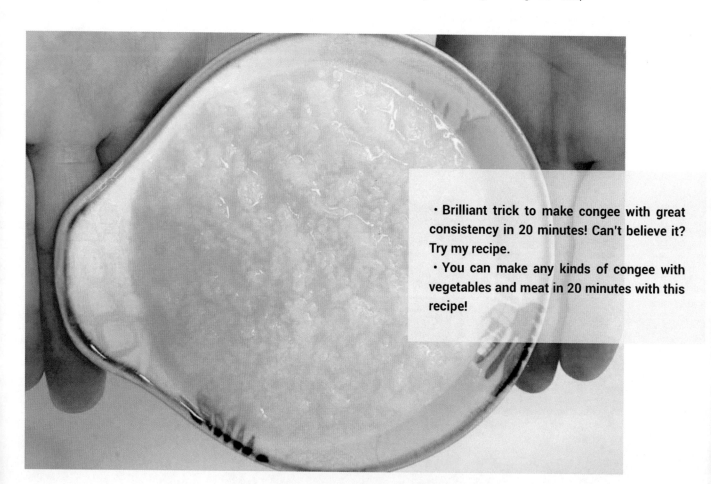

• Brilliant trick to make congee with great consistency in 20 minutes! Can't believe it? Try my recipe.
• You can make any kinds of congee with vegetables and meat in 20 minutes with this recipe!

Ingredients:

★1 cup rice
★8 cups water

Instructions for Cooking Over the Stove Top:

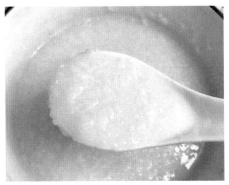

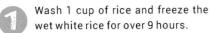 Wash 1 cup of rice and freeze the wet white rice for over 9 hours.

② Take out the frozen rice and transfer to the soup pot with 8 cups of water.

③ Bring water and rice to a boil, stirring the rice to prevent sticking. Reduce heat to a low simmer, Cover and cook for about 15 minutes, stirring the congee every few minutes to prevent from sticking on the bottom.

④ When the congee is cool enough to eat, you would find it's the perfect consistency you want!

Instructions for Instant Pot:

① Wash 1 cup of rice and freeze the wet white rice for over 9 hours.(Don't drain well...it needs a little water)

② Take out the frozen rice and transfer to the instant pot with 8 cups of water.

③ Put on lid and set vent to "seal." Push the "porridge" button for 20 minutes of pressurized cook time.

④ When the congee is cool enough to eat, you would find it's the perfect consistency you want!

Tips

◆ The perfect proportion of rice and water is 1:8. But if you want thin congee, you can add more water(about 1-2 cups).

◆ As the congee cools, it will become thicker. Add additional water if necessary to make the congee to your desired thickness.

◆ You can make any kinds of congee with vegetables and meat in 20 minutes with this recipe. Add marinated minced meat 6-8 minutes before the congee is done. Add the vegetables 3-4 minutes before the congee is done.

◆ How to marinate the 5oz meat(chicken or pork) for congee: Chop the meat into small pieces (about pea size).Marinate the meat: Put the meat in a bowl, mix well with 1 teaspoon shaoxing wine or dry sherry, 1 teaspoon light soy sauce and 1 teaspoon of dark soy sauce.

Pork Congee with Century Egg

Prep
15 mins

Cooking
1 hour

Total
75 mins

- It's the only congee that I want to recommend and share.
- You can find it anywhere if there is a congee restaurant because it has so many fans in China.
- Congee is a rice porridge that has thousands of years of history in Chinese culture.

Ingredients:

★5 oz Pork (lean meat)

★1 century duck egg

★1 bowl of pak choi

★1 teaspoon sliced ginger

★1 cup of rice

★8 cups of water

★1/2 teaspoon salt

★1 teaspoon sesame oil (optional)

Marinade pork ingredients

★1 teaspoon light soy sauce

★1 teaspoon dark soy sauce

★1 teaspoon Shaoxing wine
  (or dry sherry) optional

Tips

◆ The perfect proportion of rice and water is 1:8. But if you want thin congee, you can add more water (about 1-2 cups)

◆ As the congee cools, it will become thicker. Add additional water if necessary to make the congee to your desired thickness.

◆ It's made in instant pot. You can also make it by pot in 20 minutes; read my 20 minute congee recipe.

Instructions:

1 Chop the pork into small pieces (about pea size). Marinate the pork: Put the pork in a bowl, mix well with 1 teaspoon light soy sauce, 1 teaspoon shaoxing wine and 1 teaspoon dark soy sauce. Set aside.

2 Wash the rice , drain well and put in the instant pot with 8 cups of water. Press the "porridge" button to begin cooking (no need to adjust the time or pressure).

3 Chop the century egg and cut the pak choi into 2-3 parts. (The century egg is sticky inside to chop. You can steam it for 8 minutes under medium heat, then it will not be sticky).

4 20 minutes before the congee is ready(the display of instant pot would show the time), add the pork, chopped century egg and 1/2 teaspoon salt to the congee, and stir slowly. Close the instant pot.

5 5 minutes before the congee is ready, add the pak choi to the congee and stir.

6 When the congee is ready, sprinkle the scallions, add the sesame oil, and serve warm.

Chinese Tea Eggs

Prep
5 mins

Cooking
10 mins

Total
15 mins (not including the soak time)

One of the most famous street food and breakfast in China.

Ingredients:

★4 eggs

★2 teaspoons dark soy sauce

★2 teaspoons light soy sauce

★3-5 rock sugar (optional)

★2 star anise

★2 bay leaves

★1 teaspoon salt

★1 stick Chinese cinnamon

★2 dried chilies(optional)

★2 tablespoons green tea or black tea(or two tea bags)

★Water as needed

Instructions:

1. Wash the eggs and then place in a deep pot. Add enough water to cover. Simmer the eggs with medium fire for 6-8 minutes. Transfer to cold or chilled water to cool down and then crack the eggs carefully with a scoop.

3. Soak overnight covered with lid. (For soft boiled eggs, do not cover but wait until the liquid becomes room temperature and then soak the eggs overnight covered with lid.)

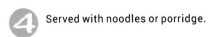

2. Add all seasonings (bay leaves, star anise, Chinese cinnamon, dried chili, salt, sugar, tea leaves,) to the pot with 2 teaspoons light soy sauce, 2 teaspoons dark soy sauce, and simmer for 10 minutes under a low-medium heat. Turn off the heat.

4. Served with noodles or porridge.

Classic Egg Fried Rice

Prep
5 mins

Cooking
10 hours

Total
15 mins

A great way to use leftover rice. Classic is classic. It's my secret recipe for fried rice. Everyone in my family LOVES it so much!

Ingredients:

★2 tablespoons cooking oil

★2 eggs

★2 scallions(chopped)

★2 bowls of leftover rice or cold rice

★12-25 garlic cloves(minced) (The more , the better . Trust me)

★2 teaspoons light soy sauce

★1/2 teaspoon salt , or to taste

Instructions:

1 Finely mince the garlic cloves and chop the scallions.

2 Heat up the wok or a frying pan on medium heat with 2 tablespoons oil, after about 45 seconds(heat the oil), then add garlic cloves; stir-fry for about 1 minute until smells fragrant, then add the rice. Stir-fry for about 3 minutes, separate the rice grains. (I love chopsticks to stir).

3 Break 2 eggs in the rice and stir-fry for another 5 minutes until the eggs become solid. Add 2 teaspoons light soy sauce and 1/2 teaspoon salt. Give them a quick stir for about 5-8 minutes until the rice grains are dry enough. Sprinkle the scallions.

4 Taste before dish out!

Tips

◆ Minced garlic cloves are the soul of this easy fried rice. So using more minced garlic cloves would make a huge difference.

◆ The leftover rice should be dry. Otherwise it takes much longer time to stir-fry.

◆ It is 100% necessary to prepare the rice a day ahead of time. That extra day is everything to this recipe.

Fried Rice Restaurant Style (with Shrimps)

Prep
15 mins

Cooking
10 mins

Total
25 mins

A star dish throughout all restaurants in China.
Whenever I don't know what to order in restaurants, it is always a wise choice.

Ingredients:

★2 tablespoons cooking oil

★2 eggs

★2 scallions (chopped)

★2 bowls of leftover rice or cold rice

★1/2 carrot

★1 bowl of peas

★1/3 bowl of shrimps

★6 garlic cloves (minced)

★1 teaspoon light soy sauce

★1/2 teaspoon salt , or to taste

★1 teaspoon dark soy sauce

★1 teaspoon oyster sauce or sugar (optional, if you like a little bit sweet)

Marinate shrimp ingredients:

★1 teaspoon shaoxing wine or dry sherry

★1/2 teaspoon sliced ginger

★1 teaspoon cornstarch

★1 teaspoon ground black pepper

★1/2 teaspoon salt

Instructions:

1 Finely mince the garlic cloves and chop the scallions and carrot. Marinate the shrimps: Clean the shrimp and put in a bowl. Mix well with 1 teaspoon shaoxing wine or dry sherry, 1 teaspoon cornstarch, 1/2 teaspoon salt, 1 teaspoon ground black pepper, and 1/2 teaspoon sliced ginger. Set aside for 10 minutes.

2 Blanch the peas and carrot: Boil a bowl of water in the wok, add the peas and carrots after the water boils; take them out after 30 seconds. Cool with temperature water, then drain them well. Set aside.

3 Heat up the wok or a frying pan to a medium heat with 2 tablespoon oil for about 45 seconds(heat the oil), then add garlic cloves; stir -fry for about 50 seconds until fragrant. Then add the shrimps and a teaspoon dark soy sauce.

4 Stir-fry until the shrimps change color, add the peas, carrots and a teaspoon oyster sauce. Stir-fry for less than 1 minute; add the rice , stir fry about 3 minutes. (I love chopsticks to stir)

5 Break 2 eggs in the rice and stir-fry for another 5 minutes until the eggs become solid. Add 1 teaspoon light soy sauce and 1/2 teaspoon salt. Give them a quick stir for about 3 minutes until the rice grains are dry enough. Sprinkle the scallions.

6 Taste before dishing out!

Tips

Restaurants would definitely to use high heat to fry. But i don't recommend you to use high heat first, because it is quite easy to burn the ingredients.

Simplest Scallion Egg Pancakes - The Chinese Breakfast of Champions

Prep
5 mins

Cooking
10 mins

Total
15 mins

Every time I am hurry for making breakfast or dinner for my daughter, this always my first choice because it's so simple, quick, and super yummy!

Ingredients:

★6 tablespoons all-purpose flour

★3 eggs

★5 scallions(chopped)

★1/2 carrot(optional)

★1 teaspoon salt(or to taste)

★1 teaspoon light soy sauce

★12 tablespoons water

★8-10 tablespoons cooking oil(divided)

Instructions:

① Finely mince the carrot and chop the scallions.

② Prepare a big bowl. Mix all the ingredients: 6 tablespoons all purpose flour, 1 teaspoon salt, 1 teaspoon light soy sauce, 12 tablespoons water, 3 eggs , carrot and scallions. Whisk to incorporate.

③ Heat a nonstick pan(4.75 inch) with 1 tablespoon cooking oil for about 20 seconds; pour about 1.5oz batter to the pan, swirling as you do to coat the bottom. Cook for about 2 minutes, until the top has set. Flip the pancake to the other side until the top has set. Place on a plate.

④ Usually you can make 8-10 small pancakes. Serve warm or cold. (I like to eat cold pancakes but my husband likes the warm.)

Tips

◆ The first secret is the pan. I love using small sized nonstick pan to make pancakes. Much easier to control both the pan and pancakes.

◆ The second secret is the thickness of pancakes. Remember the perfect proportion of flour and water is 1:2.

◆ The third secret is the salt. This pancake tastes better if it is a bit salty. You can taste in step 2.

Homemade Chili Oil

Prep
5 mins

Cooking
10 mins

Total
15mins

Spicy people are crazy about it. Whatever they have rice, noodles,or dumplings , they can not live without it.

Instructions:

Ingredients:

★8 tablespoons cooking oil (divided) (sesame oil is better)

★1 bunch of cilantro

★3-5 star anise

★1 cinnamon stick (preferably cassia cinnamon)

★4 bay leaves

★Half of an onion

★1 sprig green onion

★1 teaspoon sliced ginger

★1 tablespoon black or white sesame seed

★2 tablespoons crushed red pepper flakes or powder

★1 teaspoon salt (to taste)

1 Slice the onions , green onion and ginger Clean the cilantro and drain well.

2 Prepare a bowl. Mix well 2 tablespoons crushed red pepper flakes, 2 tablespoons oil, a teaspoon salt and 1 tablespoon black sesame seed.

4 Fry these ingredients for about 10 minutes until they got a little bit burned. (the surface of them begin to turn gold color) The whole process of frying smells so fragrant. Even the people who do not like spicy are surprised by the smell.

3 Heat the 6 tablespoons oil with the wok for 30 seconds on a medium heat (don't make the oil too hot). Add the sliced ginger, onion, green onion, star anise, cinnamon stick, bay leaves and cilantro to stir fry. Turn to the low heat.

5 Take out the ginger, onion, spring onion, star anise, cinnamon stick, bay leaves, and cilantro out, and pour the hot oil to the bowl. Mix well.

Chapter 8
Soup

only share 2 soup recipes: One is Tomato Egg Drop Soup, which is every family's favorite. The second recipe is spinach and fried egg soup; both are extremely popular in China.

Tomato Egg Drop Soup

Prep	**Cooking**	**Total**
5 mins	5 mins	10 mins

10 minutes soup--Lazy moms love
Super simple, super appetizing

Ingredients:

★1 tablespoon cooking oil

★1 big tomato

★2 eggs

★1 scallion (chopped)

★2 teaspoons light soy sauce

★2 bowls of boiled water

★2 bowls of room temperature water

★1/2 teaspoon salt , or to taste

How to peel tomatoes:

1 Cut a small cross on each tomato

2 Leave them under boiled water for 4-5 minutes

3 Take them out and pull the skin off when cool enough to touch, remove the stems.

Instructions:

1 Peel off the skin of the tomato. Then cut them into chunks. Break the eggs, and beat them. Finely chop the scallion.

3 Add 2 bowls of water, leave it until the water boils .Pour the eggs into the wok; stir slowly to spread the eggs. When the eggs become solid, add 1/2 teaspoon salt and 2 teaspoons light soy sauce.

4 Taste and sprinkle with the chopped scallions before dishing out.

2 Heat up the wok with a tablespoon oil for about 1 minute on a high heat, add the tomato and stir fry for a minute until the juices come out.

Tips

◆ Choose the red and ripe tomatoes. Soft ones would be better.

◆ If you prefer more juice, Longer the cooking time in step 2 of how to peel tomatoes. I always love more juice. More juice makes the soup tasty.

Spinach and Fried Egg Soup

Prep
2 mins

Cooking
20 mins

Servings
2

**Popeye would cry if he had the soup!--
Unbelievably delicious**

Ingredients:

★2 tablespoons cooking oil (divided)

★1 teaspoon sesame oil

★2 eggs

★4 oz spinach

★1 teaspoon sliced fresh ginger

★2 teaspoons light soy sauce

★2 bowls of boiled water

★1/2 teaspoon salt , or to taste

★2 bowls of water

Tips

The eggs need to be fried thoroughly.

Over easy eggs.

◆Remember add boiled water in step 4.

Instructions:

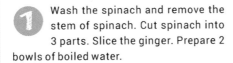

1 Wash the spinach and remove the stem of spinach. Cut spinach into 3 parts. Slice the ginger. Prepare 2 bowls of boiled water.

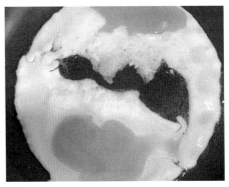

2 Heat the wok with 1 tablespoon cooking oil on a high heat. Fry 2 eggs over easy. Take out and set aside. (The eggs need to be cook thoroughly)

3 Heat another 1 tablespoon cooking oil on a medium heat for about 40 seconds, then add the spinach. Give them a quick stir-fry until the spinach begins to soften.

4 Add 2 teaspoons light soy sauce; add 2 bowls of boiled water and 2 fried eggs. Cook for 10-15 minutes; add 1/2 teaspoon salt and a teaspoon sesame oil.

5 Taste before dishing out!

Chapter 9
Chinese Steamed Buns
(Bao Zi and Man Tou)

They are both time consuming dishes to Prepare, so I share the easiest and simplest methods I have found are much trail and error.

Chinese Steamed Buns (without Fillings)-MAN TOU

Prep
1 hour 30 Mins

Cooking
20 mins

Total
1 hour 50 Mins

◆It's called Man Tou in Chinese. Actually It's the Chinese steamed buns without fillings.

◆I love using the stand mixer which makes it much easier and always makes the steamed buns much fluffier!

Ingredients: (16-20 buns depend on the size)

★18oz all-purpose flour

★9oz warm water (about 95°F)

★3oz dry yeast

Instructions:

1 Prepare a big bowl, mix 18oz all purpose flour and 3oz dry yeast. Pour 9oz warm water slowly to the bowl with flour and stir with a chopstick.

2 Then knead the flour mixture into smooth and soft dough which takes about 6 minutes. Or you can simply resort to a stand mixer(8-9 minutes).

Bring 2 bowls of water to a boil and turn the heat off . Put the bowl in for 40 minutes fermentation. (Cover with lid)

Honeycomb texture when pulled apart means fermentated well.

3 Cover the bowl and let the dough rest for around 40 minutes or until the ball doubles in size as pictured. (The first picture shows the ferment way) Don't over ferment the dough. It will be sour and takes much longer time to re-knead to remove the holes inside.

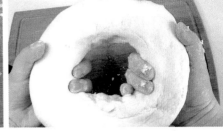

There are no large bubbles inside means re kneading is done well.

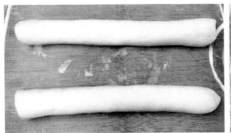

4 Get the paste ball out, dust the board and re-knead the dough for 15 minutes until the dough becomes almost smooth again. Make the dough into a round shape and dig a hole by hand in the middle (I love this way to make the dough). Cut and divide the dough into two parts, keep kneading and shape each part into 1.5 inch thick long log.

5 Then divide the dough into 16-20 portions. Second time fermentation: Place buns in the steamer, turn up the fire and heat for 2 minutes, turn off the fire and wait for 10 minutes. Then start the fire again and steam the buns for 15 minutes after the water boils. Wait for 5 minutes with lid covered and then enjoy the buns!

Tips

- ◆ It's very easy to make mistakes in step 3. Fermentation in winter is harder because you need to control the temperature for fermentation. But don't over ferment the dough, otherwise you will need long time to get the air out. It's especially easy to over ferment in summer...your dough will smell sour.
- ◆ Step 4 takes time for practicing. Remember when the dough is sticky, dust your board with flour. A long time re-kneading (10-15 minutes) will give your buns a smooth surface.
- ◆ Step 5 is necessary. It's called second time fermentation which makes your buns soft and much fluffier!

How to Make Bao zi at Home

Prep
30 mins

Cooking
40 mins

Total
70 mins

One day I brought the steamed pork buns to my family reunion party. All of them were so surprised about the taste and told me it's the best steamed pork buns!
Try my recipe, you would love it.

Fillings :

Ingredients: (16-20 buns depend on the size)

★1 tablespoon cooking oil

★10 oz Pork(choose the pork with both lean and at least 30% fatty part)

★1 teaspoon salt

★2 tablespoons light soy sauce

★2 teaspoons dark soy sauce

★1 tablespoon sesame oil

★8 fresh mushrooms

★5 scallions

★1 teaspoon minced ginger

★1 egg

Instructions:

1 Cut the pork into chunks and mince them with blender.

2 Clean the fresh mushrooms and mince them with blender. Finely mince the ginger and scallions.

3 Mix the minced ginger, scallions, mushrooms and pork. Break an egg into it; add 1 teaspoon salt, 2 tablespoons light soy sauce, 2 teaspoons dark soy sauce and 1 tablespoon sesame oil. Stir about 2 minutes to mix well. The filling is ready. Set aside.

Dough:

Ingredients:
(16-20 buns depend on the size)

★ 18oz all-purpose flour

★ 9oz warm water (about 95°F)

★ 3oz dry yeast

1 Prepare a big bowl, mix 18oz all purpose flour and 3oz dry yeast. Pour the warm water slowly to the bowl with flour and stir with a chopstick.

2 Then knead the flour mixture into smooth and soft dough which takes about 6 minutes. Or you can simply resort to a stand mixer(8-9 minutes).

Bring 2 bowls of water to a boil and turn the heat off . Put the bowl in for 40 minutes fermentation. (Cover with lid)

Honeycomb texture when pulled apart means fermentated well.

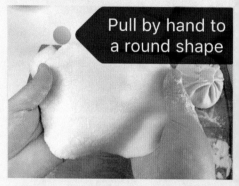
Remenber to make the centre thick and edge thin (otherwise the fillings would leak when steaming

③ Cover the bowl and let the dough rest for around 40 minutes or until the ball doubles in size as pictured (The first picture shows the ferment way). Don't over ferment the dough. It will be sour and takes much longer time to re-knead to remove the holes inside.

Pull by hand to a round shape

There are no large bubbles inside means re kneading is done well.

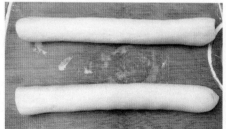

⑤ Then divide the dough into 16-20 portions. Roll each portion into a circle(You can also use your hand to make the dough, by pressing and pulling to a round shape.) Remember to make the centre thick and edge thin (otherwise the fillings would leak when steaming. Place 1 tablespoon of filling in the middle and seal it. (around 1.5 inch wide).

④ Get the paste ball out, dust the board and re-knead the dough for 15 minutes until the dough becomes almost smooth again. Make the dough into a round shape and dig a hole by hand in the middle (I love this way to make the dough). Cut and divide the dough into two parts, keep kneading and shape each part into 1.5 inch thick long log.

Steam the pork buns

Second Time Fermentation (very important step）：Place them in steamer, turn up the fire and heat for 2 minutes, turn off the fire and wait for 10 minutes. Then start the fire and steam the buns for 20 minutes after the water boils. Wait for 5 minutes with lid covered and then enjoy the pork buns!

Tips

Mushroom, scallions and ginger make the pork buns taste much better!
◆ Egg can tenderize the pork. Same amount of water also works but not as good as eggs.

2 Vegetarian Steamed Buns

Prep
30 mins

Cooking
40 mins

Total
70 mins

These are the most delicious Chinese steamed buns I have ever tasted! It's the No.1 list of my vegetarian steamed buns, so I want to share with you.

Fillings :

Ingredients: (16-20 buns depend on the size)

★10-12 oz Chinese cabbage

★4oz dried glass noodles

★1 teaspoon salt

★2 tablespoons light soy sauce

★1 teaspoon dark soy sauce

★2 teaspoons sesame oil

★4 scallions (finely chopped)

★2 teaspoons minced ginger

★3 eggs

Instructions:

1 Remove the stalk of Chinese cabbage and mince cabbage with blender. Squeeze hard(by hand) to remove the excess water. Finely mince the ginger and scallions.

2 Soak the glass noodles in the hot water(about 210 degrees) for 20 minutes. And then mince them with blender. (If too sticky to blend, use scissors to cut the glass noodles).

Make the dough, Fold and Steam Instructions are same as the pork buns instructions.

3 Break 3 eggs and whisk. Heat the pan with oil under a high heat for 1 minute and pour the eggs; stir until eggs begin to be solid and break them into small pieces.

4 Mix the minced ginger, scallions, glass noodles, Chinese cabbage and eggs. Add 1 teaspoon salt, 2 tablespoons light soy sauce, 1 teaspoon dark soy sauce and 2 teaspoons sesame oil. Stir about 2 minutes to mix well. The fillings are ready. Set aside.

Chapter 10
Dumplings and Wonton

I love to make dumplings and wonton for dinner because it takes so little time. The dumplings recipes here are the most classic in China and the ingredients are easy to find. As for the wonton recipe, you will be surprised how delicious they are! I recommend you use a blender and buy dough from the market.

1 Cabbage and Pork Dumplings

Prep
2 mins

Cooking
20 mins

Total
22 mins

No.1 popular and easy homemade dumplings in China.

the Fillings (40-50 dumplings)

Ingredients:
(16-20 buns
depend on the size)

★12 oz Cabbage

★10 oz Pork(choose the pork with
   both lean and fatty part)

★1 teaspoon salt(or to taste)

★2 tablespoons light soy sauce

★1 teaspoon dark soy sauce

★2 scallions

★1 teaspoon minced ginger

★1 egg

The cabbage has lots of water after
blending, so squeeze by both hands
to remove the water.

◆Finely minced ginger and scallions
makes the fillings fragrant , egg
makes the pork tender.

Instructions:

1 Remove the stalk of the cabbage as the picture shows. Cut them into pieces and mince the cabbage with blender(don't blend too hard). Take the cabbage out and squeeze by hand to remove the excess water. Set aside.

2 Cut the pork into chunks and mince them with blender. Finely mince the ginger and scallions. Add them to the pork and break an egg in it, mix well.

3 Mix the cabbage, pork, with a teaspoon salt, 2 tablespoons light soy sauce, 1 teaspoon dark soy sauce. Stir about 2 minutes to mix well. The filling is ready.

The Dough
(Recommend buying from the market for beginners)

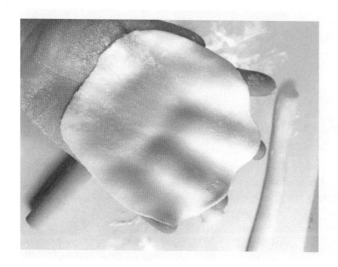

Ingredients:(40-50 wrappers)

★ 12 oz all-purpose flour

★ 5 oz warm water(about 95℉)

★ 2 tablespoons cornstarch(for dusting the board when kneading).
Cornstarch will not be absorbed as it coats the dough, creating
the perfect non-stick barrier.

Instructions:

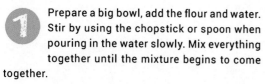

1 Prepare a big bowl, add the flour and water. Stir by using the chopstick or spoon when pouring in the water slowly. Mix everything together until the mixture begins to come together.

2 Turn the dough onto the board and knead for 3-5 minutes. The dough should be firm but silky smooth when you are done. (If your dough is too tacky, add a little extra flour to your board). Place the dough in a big bowl and cover. Let rest for 1 hour.

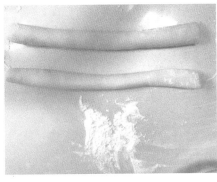

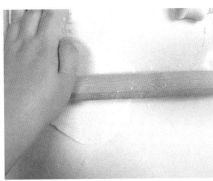
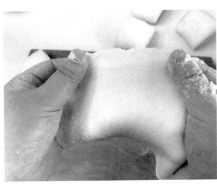

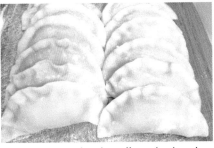

1 Wrap the dumplings by hand or by dumpling makers. Just start with a simple pattern and less filling makes your first attempts much easier. Wet the rim to make them sticky. Seal well to avoid leaking. Dust the dough and a board with flour to avoid sticking. Put the dumplings on the board.

2 Bring enough water to a boil in the wok, then add the dumplings. Stir immediately to avoid dumplings from sticking. Cook about 1 minute and add a bowl of water until boiled, then adding another bowl of water until boiled. Take the dumplings out and enjoy. (Adding 2 bowls of water to cooking dumplings is better than boiling all water from beginning which may unseal the dumplings).

3 Take the dough out, you will find it is soft and smooth now. Re-knead for about 10 minutes. Divide the dough in half. Cover one half of the dough with your towel(the dough get dry quickly in summer). Cut the dough into 10-15 portions(each one would be around 3.5 oz). Press each portion lightly first by your hand, then use the rolling pin to make it a round shape. (Sometimes the shape is not round enough, just pull it a little bit to your desired shape by your hand.)

4 Use the wrappers immediately because they will dry out quickly.

Wrapping the Dumplings and Cook Through

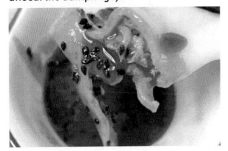

3 We love to use black vinegar to dip. But also you can use chili oil to dip.

2 Celery and Pork Dumplings

Prep
5 mins

Cooking
20 mins

Total
25 mins

Easy homemade dumplings in China

the Fillings

Ingredients:

★12 oz Celery

★14 oz Pork (choose the pork with both lean and fatty part)

★1 teaspoon salt(or to taste)

★2 tablespoons light soy sauce

★1 teaspoon dark soy sauce

★2 scallions(chopped)

★1 teaspoon minced ginger

★1 egg

Finely minced ginger and scallions makes the fillings fragrant. Egg makes the pork tender.

◆Choose the fresh and thin stalk of celery. Good celery is the soul of the dumplings.

For making the dough, folding and cooking the dumplings, read the cabbage and pork dumplings recipe.

Instructions:

1 Remove the stalk of the celery as the picture shows. Cut them into pieces and mince the celery with blender(don't blend too hard). Take the celery out and squeeze by hand to remove the excess water. Set aside. Cut the pork into chunks. Chop the scallions.

2 Finely mince the ginger, scallions and the pork. Put them in a bowl. Break an egg into it. Mix the celery and pork with 1 teaspoon salt, 2 tablespoons light soy sauce and 1 teaspoon dark soy sauce. Stir about 2 minutes to mix well. The fillings are ready.

How to Make Amazing Wonton at Home

Prep
40 mins

Cooking
1 hour and 20 Minutes

Total
2 hours

◆A wonton is a type of Chinese dumpling commonly found across regional styles of Chinese cuisine.

◆Perfect wonton soup is the soul. It took me 7 years to find the ideal and easy one to share with you.

◆Wonton is easy to make if you buy the dough. Making dough yourself takes time for practicing.

Fillings

Ingredients:
(40-50 wontons)

14 oz Pork(choose the pork with
both lean and fatty part)

1/2 teaspoon salt (or to taste)

2 tablespoons light soy sauce

1 teaspoon dark soy sauce

5 scallions(chopped)

1 teaspoon minced ginger

1 egg

Finely minced ginger and scallions
makes the fillings fragrant. Egg
makes the pork tender.

Instructions:

1 Cut the pork into chunks and mince them with blender. Finely chop the ginger and scallions.

2 Mix the minced ginger, scallions and pork. Break an egg into it; add 1/2 teaspoon salt, 2 tablespoons light soy sauce and 1 teaspoon dark soy sauce. Stir about 2 minutes to mix well. The fillings are ready.

The Dough - My secret ingredient is cornstarch.

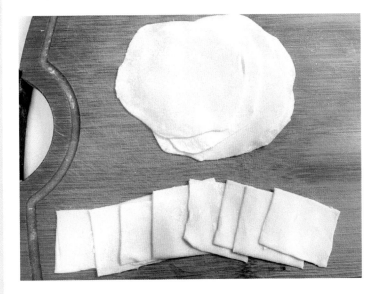

Ingredients:(40-50 wrappers)

★10 oz all-purpose flour

★4 oz warm water(about 95℉)

★2 tablespoons cornstarch(for dusting the board when kneading). Cornstarch will not be absorbed as it coats the dough, creating the perfect non-stick barrier.

Instructions:

1. Prepare a big bowl, add the flour and water. Stir by using the chopstick or spoon and pour in the water slowly. Mix everything together until the mixture begins to come together.

2. Turn the dough onto the board and knead for 3-5 minutes. The dough should be firm but silky smooth when you are done. (If your dough is too tacky, add a little extra flour to your board). Remove the dough to the big bowl and cover. Let rest for 1 hour.

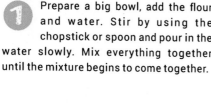

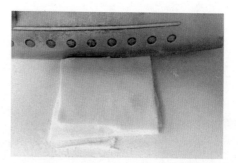

3. Take the dough out. You will find it is soft and smooth now. Re-knead for about 10 minutes. Divide the dough in half. Cover one half of the dough with your towel(the dough gets dry quickly in summer). Cut the dough into 10-15 portions(each one would be around 3 oz).

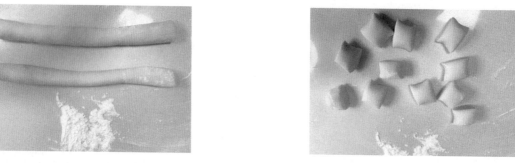

4. Lightly dust your board with cornstarch(NOT flour), and roll half of the dough as thin as you can, aiming for a rectangle roughly 20"x 10" if you are cutting 5" wrappers, or 15" x 9" if you are cutting 3" wrappers.(Dust cornstarch if your wrappers get sticky). Do the same to the remaining dough. Cut the sheet into your desired shapes. Use the wonton wrappers immediately because they will get dry soon.

Fold and Cook the Wonton

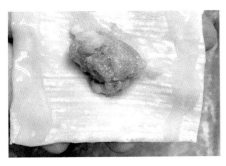 

1 Start with a simple pattern and less filling make your first attempts much easier. Wet the rim to make them sticky. Seal well to avoid leaking. Dust the dough and board with flour to avoid sticking. Put the wonton on the board. I love to fold wonton like a fish, because it is easy and pretty.

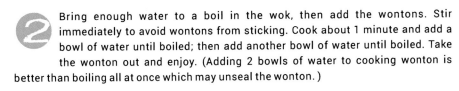

2 Bring enough water to a boil in the wok, then add the wontons. Stir immediately to avoid wontons from sticking. Cook about 1 minute and add a bowl of water until boiled; then add another bowl of water until boiled. Take the wonton out and enjoy. (Adding 2 bowls of water to cooking wonton is better than boiling all at once which may unseal the wonton.)

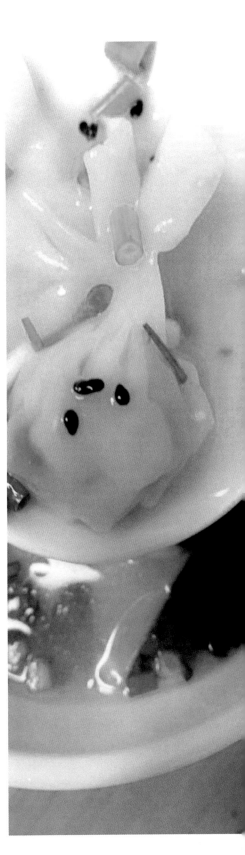

Make the Perfect Soup

Ingredients:(2 serving)

★1/2 teaspoon salt (or to taste)

★1 teaspoon light soy sauce

★1 teaspoon dark soy sauce

★1 scallion(finely chopped)

★1 teaspoon sesame oil

★1/2 teaspoon ground pepper

★1 teaspoon black or white sesame seeds

★2 pieces of nori (optional)

★2 bowls of boiled water(better use the water of boiled wonton)

Instructions:

 Prepare a big bowl, add all the ingredients then add the boiled water and stir well.

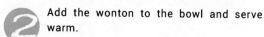 Add the wonton to the bowl and serve warm.